How To Become A

Successful Young Woman

Workbook v.1

Diamond D. McNulty

ISBN-13: 978-1945318023
ISBN-10: 1945318023
"Taking Over The World" – Diamond McNulty

Dedicated

This workbook is dedicated to all of the mothers and fathers throughout the world working hard to take care of their children. This book is also dedicated to all the children striving to become great in every aspect of life. I am here to guide you in any way possible so that you can become successful and accomplish the things that have never been done before. It takes a village to raise a child, so I am looking for every parent, guardian, brother, sister, aunt, uncle, mentor and neighbor to step up to the plate and assist in any way possible. Every child needs a positive influence for success. Stay Blessed!

"Giving visions to the youth – Spreading love to the world"

– Diamond McNulty

WELCOME

Welcome to the "How To Become A Successful Young Woman Workbook". I created this workbook based off of my own personal life plan that developed me into who I am today. This workbook will help you develop your personal success plan and give you a head start on the right path to your future. Success is not easy, but remember with the right plan in place you can truly achieve anything you set out to achieve. Before you start this workbook I would like for you to read and sign the pledge below.

MY SUCCESS PLEDGE

Dear Diamond D. McNulty, I _____ am serious about following my dreams in life. I promise to work hard, stay positive and let nothing stop me from becoming the best me. My motivation is _____ and for that reason alone I will never give up. I understand that knowledge is the key that will open doors. I will appreciate those who open doors for me and I will open doors for those who come after me. I love myself and I will never do anything to jeopardize me, my family or anyone close to me. I will write down all my goals and create my full plan to become successful because I believe that dreams do come true and that I will become successful.

_____   _____
Print: Date:

_____
Signature:

_____
Witness:

Please take a photo of this page after signing, then post and tag us on our Facebook page at www.facebook.com/successfulyoungwoman with #SuccessfulYoungWoman #IamSuccessful #TheBeginningOfMySuccessJourney

RESEARCH NOTES

Name: _____ Age: ____ Today's Date: _____

Email: _____ City/State: _____

Success Plan Worksheet

1. Name (3) things you want to become in life? (*Use only 1 sports related career*)

   a) _____

   b) _____

   c) _____

2. Name (3) things you like to do as hobbies? (*These hobbies can potentially make for great revenues streams.*)

   a) _____

   b) _____

   c) _____

3. Name (3) High Schools or Colleges you want to attend? (Don't Ask Parent)

   1. _____

   2. _____

   3. _____

4. How much money do you want to make when you get older? (Go Big!)

   a) $_____.

5. Name (6) reasons (WHY) you want to make (4.a) _____.

RESEARCH NOTES

1. _____

2. _____

3. _____

4. _____

5. _____

6. _____

6. Name (3) companies you would like to work for? Own? Why? (Look up companies that match your answers to question #1.)

1. _____.

    a. Why?

    _____
    _____.

2. _____.

    a. Why?

    _____
    _____.

3. _____.

    a. Why?

    _____
    _____.

7. What dream car do you want to have when you get older? How much does it cost? (Dream Big – Research the Internet)

    a) _____.

    Cost $ _____.

RESEARCH NOTES

How To Become A Successful Young Woman Workbook | 2016

8. How will you buy your dream car when you get older? (Circle)

    a) Cash
    b) Credit

    Explain why:

    _____

    _____

    _____

9. What size house/condo would you like to live in?

    _____

10. How many houses/condo would you like to have?

    _____

11. What are your (3) favorite classes in school? Why?

    a) _____ class.

       i. Why? _____

           _____

    b) _____ class.

       ii. Why? _____

           _____

    c) _____ class.

       iii. Why? _____

RESEARCH NOTES

12. Name (3) of your favorite books you've read?

    a) _____

    b) _____

    c) _____

13. Name (3) books you would like to read?

    a) _____

    b) _____

    c) _____

14. How many Mentors do you have? _____. Name them below and their

profession. (If you do not have one a establish one.)

    a) _____

    Profession _____

    b) _____

    Profession _____

    c) _____

    Profession _____

RESEARCH NOTES

EXERCISE

How will you become successful? (Go To …, Purchase…, Connect with…, Move to …, etc.) List out all the steps it will take you starting from today to become successful in the future.

Riches don't respond to wishes. – NAPOLEON HILL

START

1) _____

2) _____

3) _____

4) _____

5) _____

6) _____

7) _____

8) _____

9) _____

10) _____

11) _____

12) _____

13) _____

14) _____

15) _____

16) _____

17) _____

RESEARCH NOTES

18) _____

19) _____

20) _____

21) _____

22) _____

23) _____

24) _____

25) _____

26) _____

27) _____

28) _____

29) _____

30) _____

31) _____

32) _____

33) _____

34) _____

35) _____

SUCCESSFUL END – GREAT JOB!

<u>DEFINE</u>

50 WORDS EVERY SUCCESSFUL PERSON SHOULD KNOW

VOCABULARY WORD	DEFINITION
1. SUCCESS	
2. DEBT	
3. GOALS	
4. FAME	
5. WEALTH	
6. RICH	
7. POOR	
8. POVERTY	
9. DEFEAT	
10. WIN	
11. LOSE	
12. YACHT	
13. MANSION	

14.	MOTIVATION	
15.	ENTREPRENEUR	
16.	OWNER	
17.	MATERIALISTIC	
18.	PATIENCE	
19.	BOSS	
20.	SACRIFICES	
21.	WISDOM	
22.	VENTURE CAPITALIST	
23.	STOCK MARKET	
24.	RESPONSIBLE	
25.	LAZY	
26.	NEGATIVE	
27.	POSITIVE	
28.	HARD WORKING	
29.	DILIGENT	

30.	POTENTIAL	
31.	ACTION	
32.	WORK ETHIC	
33.	LIKE MINDED	
34.	CHOICE	
35.	FAITH	
36.	DEPRESSED	
37.	PROCRASTINATE	
38.	INDIFFERENT	
39.	FAILURE	
40.	COMPETITION	
41.	DOMINATE	
42.	MONEY	
43.	DISTRACTION	
44.	FOCUSED	
45.	PURPOSE	

46. AVERAGE	
47. MASSIVE	
48. CONFIDENT	
49. PROBLEM	
50. GREATNESS	

IN ORDER TO WIN YOU MUST BE FULLY PREPARED FOR SUCCESS

HOW TO ESTABLISH A DEBT FREE LIFESTYLE

1. When does most debt occur for young adults?
   a. 8th Grade
   b. High School
   c. College
   d. Graduate School

2. If you selected college you are correct. Circle all the ways to prevent occurring debt in college. (Research your answer)
   a. No Credit Cards
   b. Student Loans
   c. Create a sensible budget
   d. Get a part-time job
   e. All of these above

3. Name five additional cause of debt?
   1) _____
   2) _____
   3) _____
   4) _____
   5) _____

4. Name five ways to overcome the debt in question #3
   1) _____
   2) _____
   3) _____
   4) _____
   5) _____

RESEARCH NOTES

5. Can you live without debt? Yes or No.

    a. If circled Yes, explain how someone can live without debt.

    b. If circled No, define Financial Literacy and Money Management below.

_____

_____

_____

_____

_____

_____

_____

_____

_____

_____

_____

Note: Cash is King – If you have cash you don't need credit.

EXPENSE SCRATCH SHEET

How to create a LOW EXPENSE Budget

How much per month do you spend?

1. Cell phone _____ (Avg. Cost $70 – High)

2. Cable _____ (Avg. Cost $123 – Good)

3. Hair Done _____ (Avg. Cost $65 – Good)

4. Groceries _____ (Avg. Cost $100 a week – High)

5. Eating Out _____ (Avg. Cost $100 a mos. – Ok)

6. Books _____ (Avg. Cost $15 – Good)

7. Clothes _____ (Avg. Cost $100 a mos. - Good)

8. Shoes _____ (Avg. Cost $65 – Good)

9. Rent or Mortgage _____ (Varies by State)

10. Extracurricular activities:

    _____

    _____

11. Other_____ $_____

12. Other_____ $_____

13. Other_____ $_____

14. Other_____ $_____

Total Expenses $_____

Monthly Income (Yourself) $_____

Monthly Income (Guardian) $_____

_____ - _____ = _____

(Total Income)   (Total Expenses)   (Total Net Gross)

ADDITIONAL WORKSPACE

Let's Dig Deeper

1. Do you believe you can become successful? Yes or No.

    Explain:_____

    _____

    _____.

2. What obstacles do you face that could stop you from becoming successful?

    a) _____

    b) _____

    c) _____

2a. What measures are you putting in place to prevent from failing?

_____

_____

_____

_____

_____

_____.

3. Do you have any bad habits? If so, write down the bad habit(s) and give it an expiration date.

    a) _____ Expiration Date:_____

    b) _____ Expiration Date:_____

    c) _____ Expiration Date:_____

ADDITIONAL WORKSPACE

4. Do you have any positive role models around you? Yes or No.

   If yes, name them below:

   a) _____

   b) _____

   c) _____

   If no, find (3) positive role models that you can look up to and write them below:

   a) _____

   b) _____

   c) _____

4b. Identify the positive qualities of these individuals and how those qualities can assist you in becoming successful?

_____

_____

_____

_____

_____

5. Do your teachers care about you? Yes or No

   a. If yes, proceed to question #6.

   b. If no, do not let that stop you from pursuing your dreams on becoming successful, stay focused.

6. What do you feel you are missing that could help you become successful?

   a) _____

   b) _____

   c) _____

ADDITIONAL WORKSPACE

6b. How are you planning on obtaining what is missing? (Establish a realistic deadline for each.)

a) _____. Deadline to obtain: _____

b) _____. Deadline to obtain: _____

c) _____. Deadline to obtain: _____

7. What are your biggest fears?

a) _____

b) _____

c) _____

7b. How do you plan on overcoming fears:

a) _____

b) _____

c) _____

8. Do you feel your school is preparing you to become successful? Yes or No.

   a. If Yes, explain.

   b. If No, what can you do to help prepare yourself?

_____

_____.

9. Are there any negative things going on around you on a daily basis?

a) _____

b) _____

c) _____

ADDITIONAL WORKSPACE

9b. Write down how you can overcome those negative things.

a) _____

b) _____

c) _____

10. Write a 1-page paper about where you see yourself in 5-years.

ADDITIONAL WORKSPACE

Where I am and where I want to be!

START POINT - A
As of today.

Name:
Age:
Date:
City:
State:
Country:

What school do you attend?

What is your current job?

What is your current salary per year?

Are you single or in a relationship? Yes or No. If yes, can you see yourself married to her?

Do you have kids? Yes or No. If yes, how many?

How many Entertainment Oriented friends do you have?

How many Business Oriented friends do you have?

Do you have a Bank Account? Yes or No.

Do you have a Savings Account? Yes or No.

Do you have a car? If yes, make and model?

ADDITIONAL WORKSPACE

Have you burned any bridges? If yes, please explain.

_____

_____

_____

_____

_____

Do you have any court cases against you? Yes or No.

What are (3) of your biggest motivations to become successful?

1._____

2._____

3._____

Do you believe you can become successful? Yes or No.

If yes, how will you become successful? If no, why not?

_____

_____

_____

Indicate (2) backup plans.

_____

_____

_____

_____

_____

_____

SUCCESS PLAN SCRATCH SHEET

List Short Term Goals
Within The Next 5 Years

<u>ADDITIONAL WORKSPACE</u>

List Long Term Goals
Within The Next 10 Years +

ADDITIONAL WORKSPACE

END POINT- B

Predict your future 10 years from now.

Name:
Age:
Date:
City:
State:
Country:

What is your current career?

What is your current salary per year?

Are you single, in a relationship or married?

Who is in your Network (Trust Circle)?

_____

_____

_____

_____

_____

Do you have kids? Yes or No. If yes, how many?

How many Entertainment Oriented friends do you have?

How many Business Oriented friends do you have?

Do you have a bank and savings account? If yes, how many?

Do you have a car? Yes or No. If yes, make and model?

<u>SUCCESS PLAN SCRATCH SHEET</u>

Have you burned any bridges? If yes, please explain.

_____

_____

_____

Have you accomplished all your goals? Yes or No. If yes, list them.

_____

_____

_____

What are (3) of your biggest motivations to become successful?

1._____

2._____

3._____

Are you successful so far? If yes, explain.

_____

_____

_____

Did you have to implement a backup plan? If yes, was it successful? Explain.

_____

_____

_____

Will you look to become more successful? Explain.

_____

_____

_____

SUCCESS PLAN SCRATCH SHEET

VISION BOARD
"Taking Over The World"

As a part of the success plan, I will help you create your vision board. I want you to go to your nearest store and pickup (1) dry erase board, (1) dry board erase marker, (1) medium poster board, (1) glue stick or pack of tape, (1) pair of scissors, (1) map of the world and a few old newspapers and magazines. I want you to answer each question below on the dry erase board and then place it on your wall in your room. On the poster board, now your 'vision board' you can either write the things you want to accomplish or glue pictures of the things you want to accomplish to it and place it somewhere in your room so you can see it every day. Also, hang the map on your wall wherever you can see it every day, to motivate you to take over the world.

1. What do you want to be in life?
   a. *Doctor, lawyer, Political Figure, Entrepreneur, Sports Owner, etc....*

2. What do you want to accomplish in your life time?
   a. *Win Awards, Buy a house, Car, Travel, Kids, Spouse*

3. How will you make a difference in society?
   a. *Give back to the youth? Become a volunteer, mentor, donate?*

4. Name every material thing you want? Price it?

5. Name everything you need to accomplish your goals? Price it?
   a. *(Clothes, Computer, Gadgets, TVs, Piano, Etc....)*

6. What schools will you attend? College? Graduate School Etc....?

7. What are the best places to do internships for your career?

8. Places you would love to travel?

9. Hobbies you will like to acquire?

10. Write 3 books you would like to read?

ADDITIONAL WORKSPACE

VISION BOARD

WORKSPACE

ADDITIONAL WORKSPACE

ADDITIONAL WORKSPACE

Congratulations on your new

journey to Becoming A Successful Young Woman, I wish
you all the success in the world!

To download your Certificate of Completion please visit:

www.successfulyoungwoman.com

Visit the following website for more information on seminars and appearances:
www.mcnultyinternational.com

To contact us for more information:
E-mail: info.mcnultyinternational@gmail.com
(404) 850 – 7947

www.ingramcontent.com/pod-product-compliance
Lightning Source LLC
Chambersburg PA
CBHW081158090426
42736CB00017B/3378

9781945318023